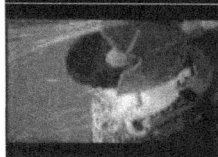
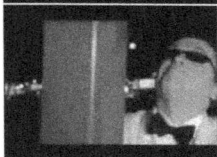

FORMULAIC
How to Make a Brand Truly Great

Printed in the United States of America

Published by Penny Arcades Press, 5030 Champion Blvd. G11-401, Boca Raton FL 33496

FIRST EDITION APRIL 2019

The body of this book is typeset using Dr. Edmond Arnold's typography studies of optimized pica line length with CORONA as the body text and OPTIMA as the heads.

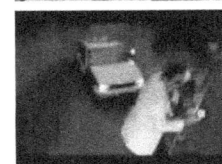

Contents

Part 1: Understanding Brands..........................1
  One Word 1
  The Success & Failure of Neighbors 2
  Ashtrays and Cufflinks..................................4
  The Power of a BRAND 8
  Goal *vs* Tasks and 'Ars Gratia Artis' 13
  Sustainable Competitive Advantage 20
  Why Good Brands Go Bad...........................23
Part 2: Projecting Earnings...........................25
  It Is Not Experiment-driven 25
  Revenue Sources..28
  Transforming a Brand to Revenue................31
  Creating Economies of Scale 32
Part 3: Increase & Track Revenue 35
  20 Questions Toward Branding 35
  The Secret of RFM.......................................44
Part 4: Changing markets 51
  Setting Data-Driven Activity 51
  Henny Penny, Chicken Little, Baby Boomers, and
  Millennials 52
  Panic vs. Data 54
Part 5: Making a Brand Great 56
  From Loyalty to Revenue Projections 56
  The Branding Paradigm for Revenue...............61
Other Books By Gary Green............................63

Part 1: Understanding Brands
One Word

There is a great scene from the 1981 Warren Beatty film, *Reds*, in which Beatty's character is asked to speak to a stodgy meeting of his parent's political club in Portland. Warren plays the activist-journalist John Reed, who had just returned from a writing assignment on the front lines of the first World War.

In the scene, he is attending a luncheon meeting at the club; of no interest to him at all, but as a good son's favor to his mother.

After a few spirited speeches debating the causes of the Great War, the chairman of the political club called impromptu on the young writer, announcing, "tonight we have with us the son of Margaret and the late C.J. Reed of Portland, who has witnessed this war first-hand. And I, for one, see no reason why we here shouldn't listen to what Jack Reed has to say. What would you say this war is about, Jack Reed?"

The crowd settled back, prepared to hear another stirring patriotic speech; this one from the young battlefield-returned writer.

Instead, the young man stood, straightened his suit and tie, walked to the front of the room (stopping to shake a few hands on the long walk from the back of the hall), slowly climbed the three steps to the stage, took a few strides across the stage to the podium, cleared his throat, and with exaggerated effort and pseudo-thoughtfulness took hold of the lectern and said, "Profits."

After uttering that one word, he stepped off the stage, walked back through the hall, and returned to his seat at the table at the back of the room. The crowd gasped, with most people unsure how to react.

Simple and to the point.

Since seeing that film almost three decades ago, I have often wondered if there is some equally snarky one-word response that I can offer when people ask me "what is marketing all about"? There is: *"formulaic"*.

The Success & Failure of Neighbors

I n the casino world, think about it, we all have the same slot machines. Within the regulated parameters, the payout is the same; in "Class II casinos" the payouts are almost identical. The table games are the same and the odds of winning are the same. We all have buffets, a gourmet room, cocktail waitresses, entertainment. We even have basically the same ugly carpet on our floors. We all have players' clubs. As incestuous as this industry is, even our employees are interchangeable; especially our General Managers.

At the end of the day what makes one casino successful and the one nearby a failure?

- So why is it that in Vegas, one casino's recent EBITDA was $57.4-million and the casino literally next door earned $87.2-million, while a third casino, on the other side next door, lost $56-million?
- Why is it that in Atlantic City, recently, one casino's gaming revenue was $55.5-million and 2½-miles away another casino's revenue was $10.7-million for the same month?

- Why, in the same timeframe, did one Florida casino make $10.3-million and a second one with an identical number of games and in the same county made only $4.5-million?

With geographic access and all physical contingencies being equal, is it even possibly be as simple as <u>customer reaction to Branding</u>?

Actually, the answer to that is... YES.

Gaming is a highly formulaic business. Financial results can be projected with a high degree of accuracy and reliability by understanding and adhering to specific formulaic methodologies that repeatedly have proven to accurately project, track, and actually increase revenue.

Strict adherence to these formulas will transform a generic or mediocre Brand into a truly great Brand.

Ashtrays and Cufflinks

A few years ago, I took over management of a large but money-losing casino. To begin the turnaround process, I called a meeting of the entire staff, all four shifts, to talk about the issues.

One of the first questions I asked was, "I want to know who our best customer is. Who can tell me about our best coverage?"

Dead silence. No takers. So, I pleaded, "come on, someone raise your hand and tell me who our best customer is."

After a few seconds, one of the people in the marketing department raised a hand and said, "well our best customer is probably a white female between the age of 55 and 70 with a fixed retirement income and..."

I cut off the demographic recitation. "No, no, no. I want to know the NAME of our best customer. I want to know specifically who our best customer is. Who can tell me that person's name?"

More silence. Finally, after what seemed like an eternity of silence, a very shy young woman near the front of the room raised her hand and spoke. "Well, that would be Mr. Johnson, Bryan Johnson. He comes in on Wednesday and Thursdays and stays for about four hours. He plays maximum bet on the Wheel of Fortune machines near the bingo hall. He comes back in on Saturdays too, but Mrs. Johnson is with him then, so he only comes for lunch and only bets $20 total on Saturdays. He doesn't want her to know how much he gambles. Besides him, I think our next best player is Laura King and those ladies from the retirement home that come in with her every week."

THAT was the answer I was looking for; that was what I wanted to hear. That was an on-the-floor, customer-engagement, answer.

So, in which marketing department did she work? Players Club? Data analytics? Player development / hosting? Advertising? Promotions?

Nope. She cleaned ashtrays and toilets for a living. She worked in housekeeping. Well, she did up until that meeting; the next morning she started work in the marketing department.

Typically casino guests only have contact with a few employees.

Every employee of every department must essentially become a marketing employee

Typically, casino guests only see a handful of employees: housekeeping; security; maybe a dealer (if they play tables); maybe a cashier (if they don't use kiosks); maybe a greeter or a host (if the casino has them); valets; bellhops; slot attendants; and so on. At most properties, customers rarely (if ever) see the General Manager, Marketing VP (or Director), Slot Manager, or any of the back-of-the-house staff.

Consequently, front-line employees are the face of the business. Front-line employees are the face-to-face marketers of the casino.

That is not an unheard-of model; in fact, it is THE model of some of the most successful customer-centric businesses in the world.

The Red-Light Paradigm

One day, back in the 1990's, I was sitting in the office of the president of one of the most successful retail chains in the world. We were in the midst of a relatively intense discussion about the success of his auxiliary direct marketing business.

Suddenly, and without warning, the fluorescent while lights flashed and went off. They were instantly replaced by red lights. I remember thinking that his office now looked like the bridge of the Starship Enterprise during a "red alert".

This internationally famous CEO picked up his phone, pushed a button on it, and spoke, "Good afternoon; thanks for calling. How may I help you?"

The instant he answered the phone, the lights switched by to their normal florescent white and the red was gone.

Stunned, I sat and listened as he continued, "Yes 'mam; let me check that for you."

He began typing and looking at his computer screen. An inventory page appeared on the screen and he continued to engage the caller, "Yes 'mam, we do have red ones in your size. Would you like for me to hold one for you?"

"I will have that waiting for you at the Customer Service Desk on the first floor. Could I get your name?" he began typing again.

"What time do you think you will be in? We will be expecting you," he asked and assured.

A few more words and then the conversation ended. The powerful executive turned back to continue his conversation with me.

He explained that at his company there was a rule that no one calling the store was left on hold or was subjected to more than four rings without being answered. If a fourth ring happened and there was no operator available, any employee could answer the phone.

EVERY employee in the company was trained in telephone customer service; and every employee from janitor to CEO was trained to answer the phone when the red lights flashed.

It is a system that focuses the entire organization on customer service. More importantly, it is a system that is based on the understanding that customers generate revenue for the company and therefore the business is customer dependent.

Creating a customer experience that drives repeat business and generates new customers because of the experience of others...can, within itself, become the competitive edge —the differentiator— for a company.

It can be the difference between mediocre and out-standing. It can be the Brand.

The Red-Light Paradigm

The Power of a BRAND

Kleenex. Caesars Palace. Xerox. IBM. Coca-Cola. Amazon. Walt Disney. AT&T. Trump. GE. Marlboro. Budweiser. Rolex. Is there anyone here that does not recognize these Brands?

Love them or hate them; familiar with their particulars or simply aware of them; without a doubt, Brands are a "thing" worth attention.

Consider two oat breakfast cereals: General Mills' Cheerios versus Millville Crispy Oats. Consumers prefer Cheerios 105-to-1 over the Millville product. Unlike a generic knock-off, Millville Crispy Oats cereal is owned and manufactured by General Mills, using the same ingredients, the identical formula, and baked in the same manufacturing plant as Cheerios. Yet, if offered side-by-side, consumers prefer Cheerios.

VERRRRY interesting Brand loyalty.

A Brand is more than a name; it is the total of a consumer's experiences with a product. A Brand can signify quality and inspire confidence.

I am often asked about which companies I think will do best with online casinos. My answer is always the same: "If you were a consumer, who knows nothing about the inner-workings of either the technology or of casinos, which online casino would make you feel most confident in honesty of the games and safety of your money; 'Honest Bubba's On-line Offshore Games' or 'Harrahs Online Casino'? I think the answer is obvious. In a new market, consumers feel more confidence in an established Brand."

Regardless of the underlying reality, the power of the Brand alone can drive business. Proper management of that Brand, in that "every-employee-is-a-Brand-ambassador" model, can be THE determining factor in the decision of where to spend money.

A couple of years ago I was flying from south Florida to a speaking engagement in Boston. The route took me from West Palm Beach to Atlanta for a change of planes that would take me to JFK in New York. From there, I was to change again; this time to a hopper that would take me up to Logan in Boston. Convolutedly indirect I know; but it was the only schedule available to keep me on Delta Airlines. And I was Brand-loyal.

Competitor American Airlines had a one-stop (in Charlotte) flight for about the same price; maybe $20 cheaper, but more direct. United had a one-stop through Chicago, at the same price. JetBlue had a non-stop flight from Palm Beach to Boston; considerably cheaper than the Delta two-stop flight. Scary-carrier Spirit had a non-stop at about one-third the price of the Delta route. Yet I refused any airline other than Delta.

Generally, I am a relatively rational person; so, one has to wonder what would drive me to such Brand loyalty even at significant inconvenience and increased cost.

The answer to that becomes clear when we look at my relationship with the Delta Brand and they turned it into a personal relationship.

For several years I flew more than 150 flights annually (keep in mind there are only 52 weeks in a year; so, do that math). Most of those flights were on Delta Airlines; initially not because of any loyalty to Delta, but because they had the cheapest coach-fare and most direct routes to the destinations I needed at that time.

Taking that many flights on one airline very quickly qualified me as a top-tier frequent flyer. On Delta, that meant that as a "Diamond" flyer: I always received a free upgrade to First Class when I purchased a coach ticket; I always boarded before everyone else; if no seats were available on a flight, another (non-Diamond) passenger would be bumped to give me a seat; and if a flight was late for a connection, Delta would hold my next flight (within the legal gate-time limit) for my arrival, and meet me at the arrival gate.

On that particular three-leg trip from Palm Beach to Boston, my flight from Atlanta to JFK was 20 minutes late. Even jogging between terminals, there was no way that I could have made the connection from the arriving gate to the departure gate for the commuter flight to Boston; there just wasn't enough time.

As I stepped out of the plane and onto the jetway, I spotted two uniformed Delta employees holding a sign that announced, "Delta Welcomes Gary Green".

Rather than continue along the jetway to the terminal, they escorted me down the stairway onto the tarmac where a Porsche Cayenne was waiting for me. Once inside the SUV, we sped across the tarmac toward the second terminal.

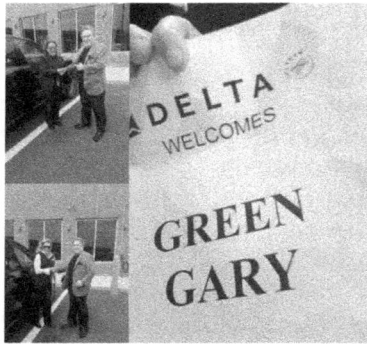

At the same time, a specially-assigned baggage handler entered the baggage-hold of the plane and retrieved my over-sized suitcase. As we drove toward the waiting Boston-bound plane, he headed to the baggage compartment of that waiting plane.

At the second terminal, the Porsche parked beside the waiting aircraft. The agent escorted me up the jetway stairs and directly into my waiting first-class seat for the short trip to Boston Logan. There was plenty of time left as other passengers continued to board from the jetway.

Besides the Porsche pickup, my "Diamond" status also meant that every year at Christmas time they sent me a $500 Tiffany gift card. It also meant that I was always upgraded to First Class even when I bought coach tickets. It meant that in addition to the full meals that everyone in First Class received, I got special amenities; a bottle of high-end champagne more than once.

One day, a few months later, I had to fly to a location that was not served by Delta. Even though I purchased a First-Class ticket on the competing airline, I felt like I had switched to a Greyhound Bus; at least in comparison to the kid-glove treatment from Delta.

In reality, it was just a typical airline — but to me, it really felt like a bus customer compared to Diamond treatment. There was no personalized service, no preboarding, no special attention, no recognition by name, and then being subjected to the indignities of crowds, long lines, and no overhead bin space.

All-in-all, changing airlines was a painful experience. It is easy to see why Delta was MY airline; no other airline would do for me the things Delta did.

Many times, I could reach the same destination faster and at a third of the price, but repeatedly I spent my money with Delta. Delta was not "an" airline; it was MY airline.

Forget loyalty; even *RECOGNITION* is powerful

In the 2016 Republican Presidential Primaries, there were 22 candidates filling the debate stage: Andy Martin, Ben Caron, Bobby Jindal, Carly Fiorina, Chris Christie, Dennis Michael Lynch, George Pataki, Jack

Fellure, Jeb Bush, Jim Gilmore, Jimmy McMillan, John Kasich, Lindsay Graham, Marco Rubio, Mark Everson, Mike Huckabee, Rand Paul, Rick Perry, Rick Santorum, Scott Walker, Ted Cruz, and Donald J. Trump.

The CBS television affiliate in Palm Beach asked me to be a color commentator during those crowded debates. During one of my on-air sessions, I challenged the news team to interview 100 random people on the street, asking each one to identify the 22 people on that list, with no prompting and no clues.

My prediction was that not one person out of the 100 would be able to identify all 22 names; but all 100 would recognize the name Donald Trump. Of course, I was correct. While some of the names scored in the 40-60% recognition range, Trump alone was universally recognized.

This was not a reflection of political preference by any means; it was simply a reflection of recognizing the Brand. It was an exercise with which I was relatively confident since I had, at least in part, helped build that Brand when it mostly was only regionally known in the Northeastern states.

Even the slightest differentiator can be the foundation for a great Brand —even if the consumer knows nothing about the product itself.

I have never been to Corning California, off of The 5 about two hours north of Sacramento. But Steve Neely, the GM of the Rolling Hills Casino for the Paskenta Band of Nomlaki Indians has added a tagline that differentiates his casino from the 573 other casinos in America: "California's Friendliest Casino."

Again, I have never been there, but you know what? I believe his tag line. I believe that Brand-tease. It makes me want to go there.

Even the most basic differentiator is a powerful first step for Branding! Though in the bigger picture, we want to move the customer from brand awareness to brand loyalty.

Goal *vs* Tasks and 'Ars Gratia Artis'

U ltimately a Brand is all about **THE** airline generically versus **MY** airline personally; or in this case THE casino versus MY casino. Moving the customer to that level of Brand loyalty is usually helped along by various promotions[1].

At the same time, the <u>Branding</u> must not be allowed to get lost in operating a <u>promotion</u>. A promotion is a process tool; not an end. Without the proper orientation, it can become a classic case of "can't see the forest for the trees".

Imagine that you are the contractor in charge of building a really nice brick house. One of the processes is unloading the bricks from the truck and getting them in position so the masonry team can build the exterior walls. The truck arrives and you have the whole crew stop what they are doing and pitch in to help laborers unload the truck. After the bricks are unloaded, everyone goes home; because they think all the work is finished.

WTF? Did they lose sight of building the house? Or did someone fail to explain the goal; fail to explain their jobs.

Unfortunately, too many times, that Branding <u>goal</u> gets lost in the excitement of the <u>task</u>; the promotion itself. That often happens when the entire organization —janitor to CEO— doesn't understand the value of that goal. Part of understanding that value is being an active part of that goal; like those department store employees.

Because so much of marketing is often copycat marketing, the underlying and long-term goal often gets lost

---

[1] Wayne D. Hoyer and Steven P. Brown, Effects of Brand Awareness on Choice for a Common, Repeat-Purchase Product, Chicago Illinois, University of Chicago Press, The Journal of Consumer Research, Volume 17 Number 2. September 1990, pp 141-148.

in the immediate gratification of the short-term goals. It is very easy to copy, and exceed, a promotion without even being aware of the underlying "big picture" — the primary goal of Branding.

To make matters worse, copycat marketing degrades from the original intent more and more with each permutation. Too many times, a promotion becomes a goal to itself; oblivious or unaware of the Branding goal or even the incremental revenue goals.

In those cases, it is not unusual for promotions to actually lose money. Any idiot can create a promotion; and unfortunately, a good number do.

I worked with a marketing director one time who was an absolute genius at creating promotions to bring people into the casino. He carefully studied what worked at other casinos. From his observations, he created new and more attention-getting promotions; far surpassing any of the competitors' promotions that he had studied.

Incredibly successful, he repeatedly brought in hundreds —sometimes a thousand— players in a day; players who ordinarily would have gone to a competing casino that day (or not gone to any casino).

His magic was his creation of a series of high-value giveaways for players club members. If you were a member of the players club all you had to do was come into the casino on a designated day (usually the slowest day of the week) and you could collect your "appreciation gift". The perceived high-value of the gift made the unscheduled casino trip appear worthwhile and actually valuable to the player.

While he had the good sense to keep the price down and the perceived value up, his good sense stopped there. In his mind, his mission (and thus his goal) was to bring bodies into the casino; and that worked. But his copycat marketing had lost sight of incremental revenue or even the Branding.

From a Branding standpoint, there was nothing consistent from one week's promotion to the next. There was no thread of a theme holding each giveaway to a Brand message.

Much more troublesome, the secondary goal of incremental revenue got lost too. He gave away prizes that encouraged people to NOT spend money in the casino.

One week he gave away a giant set of luggage; so large that it could not be carried around the casino. The customer would come into the casino, get into a line at the players' club, redeem their gift, and be given the gigantic set of luggage that they had to take to their car (because of its size). Once they hauled the heavy load through the casino and across the parking lot, a return to the casino to gamble seemed like an onerous and unnecessary task.

Another week, he gave away a 26-pound boombox. That award, too, was so large that it had to be carried out the door and through the parking garage. It just made no sense to come back into the casino after lugging the heavy box.

Ars Gratia Artis; promotio gratia promotion
PROMOTION FOR THE SAKE OF PROMOTION
Ignoring incremental revenue, it's east to draw a crowd to carry heavy gifts out the door!

From the viewpoint of bringing huge crowds into the casino, he was a genius. Masses of people showed up and waited in line for more than an hour to claim their prizes.

But once they collected their prizes, they headed directly to the door and didn't return until the next prize day. Even the simplest corrections to the debacle were repeatedly ignored... or at least were not on the radar of the marketer.

PROMOTION FOR THE SAKE OF PROMOTION

On an immediate level, and apart from that long-term vision of Branding, a promotion is a vehicle to bring in incremental revenue; money over and above what would normally be generated without the promotion. In that regard, a promotion is supposed to either bring in more people or increase the spending of the existing customers (or both).

Even in that context, though, the relationship between promotions and Branding is not complex. Promotions are a tool to create value through the Brand and to create immediate incremental revenue in the meantime. Not complex at all.

Nonetheless, being oblivious (if not ignorant) of the purpose of promotions is not unusual. If the creation of a promotion is not part of an overall Branding strategy —and if every employee is not in on the plan— it is easy to get caught up in the frenzy and excitement of a crowd-pleasing promotion.

Even more troublesome, many crowd-attracting promotions actually lose money. Often, those are the most difficult to spot if they aren't part of a Branding strategy.

Some longtime operators, like Johnny Winokur up at Washington's Shoalwater Bay Casino, have an experience-based knack of spotting money losers before they even begin. He advises that promotions should be targeted to the customer base, not the brainstorm of the marketer.

He explains, "I came into a giveaway for a great Indian Motorcycle; and incredibly valuable prize. But it failed miserably; and it was clear to me why. If you look at the customer base, they are all over 65 years old. That prize wasn't interesting to them."

"Some marketers might think it would be a great idea to give away a Mercedes or a Maserati; but here in

16

Tokeland Washington, I know that we will get a lot more participation with a giveaway of a good four-wheeler," he added, acknowledging that he would never approve such a promotion[2].

Operators of that caliber not only save Tribes tens of thousands of dollars, but also seemingly-instinctively can spot a promotion that exists for no reason other than promotion. Not every casino is fortunate enough to have a Johnny Winokur on hand, but fortunately, there are any number of formulaic tests that should be involved in a pro forma for each promotion.

Project Name	Cash Coupon Mailing
Goal	Additional visit on slow day
Target Date	Wednesday; January 16 2019
Project Description	CASH COUPONS PLAYERS CLUB MEMBERS BASED ON ADT: ○ 3,850 members received $5 coupons ○ 1,891 members received $10 coupons ○ 1,603 members received $15 coupons ○ 1,006 members received $25 coupons ○ 329 members received $50 coupons ○ 103 members received $100 coupons.
Desired Outcome	7% response
Drop Date of Mail	January 4, 2019
In-house date	January 11
Mailing Type	Monthly Calendar
Number Mailed	38,794
Test mailings	15
Response desired	2,715 players
Geographic Target	Geo-radius of 150-miles from the casino

Criteria for targeting	• Minimum $15 ADT
	• Minimum of one visit in last 12 months
	• Minimum of 2 visits during previous four months
	  • ADT of $25-$49 receives $5 playable credit
	  • ADT of $50-$74 receives $10 playable credit
	  • ADT of $75-$124 receives $15 playable credit
	  • ADT of $125-$249 receives $25 playable credit
	  • ADT of $250-$499 receives $50 playable credit
	  • ADT of $500 or greater receives $100 playable credit.

Costs	TOTAL: $163,373 • Production Mailing and printing: $58,967 • Anticipated total playable credits: $114,105 • Discount on credits (casino win based on 8¾% hold): $104,406
REVENUE PROJECTION	• Net Revenue after costs: $549,315 • Total Revenue based on ADT: $712,688 • Threshold customer reimbursement to break even: 23%
BREAK EVEN ANALYSIS	

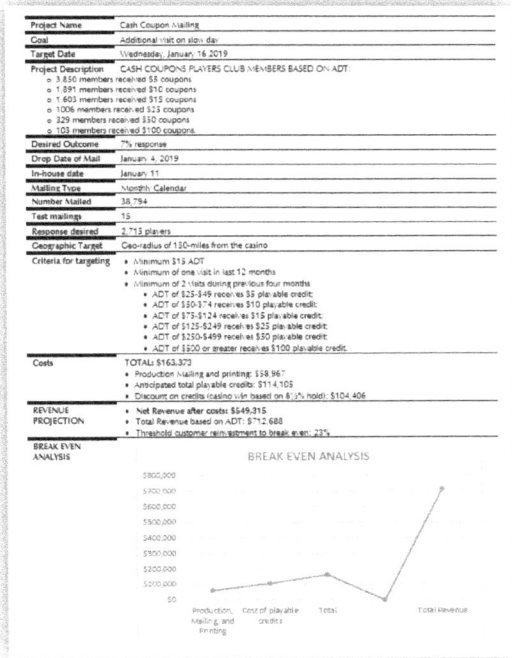

BREAK EVEN ANALYSIS

(chart with y-axis values: $800,000; $700,000; $600,000; $500,000; $400,000; $300,000; $200,000; $100,000; $0. X-axis categories: Production, Mailing and Printing; Cost of playable credits; Total; Total Revenue)

---

[2] Winokur points out that there are times that a money-losing promotion is acceptable; especially when it is being used as a "loss leader" tool to being in new customers. But he is also quick to add that a good promotion should generate significant multiples of the average revenue for the day of the promotion.

17

No promotion should ever be undertaken without a pro-forma. That exercise, even in a rudimentary cookie-cutter format, will give you at least a reasonable expectation of the costs-to-return of a promotion. Even with a gifted operator whose experience can quickly deduce the numbers, a good pro forma is important for financial projections.

One actual marketing guru and well-respected consultant, Dennis Conrad, used to compile an annual list of the Best and Worst Casino Promotions. He has a skill of ferreting out money-losing promotions; and he seemed to take glee in exposing them. At very least, he gave me great glee with his brilliant (and often hilarious) lists. More casino marketers should learn from his analytical skills.

Likewise, there are a number of companies that specialize in creating promotions that are... unlikely to be conceived by in-house marketers. Though many of those promotions are little more than "prize insurance" scams to deceive customers and protect the casino, most all of them have accurately analyzed the math to assure that the promotions don't lose money.

In fairness, many of those promotions are really effective, help build the Brand, and generate genuine measurable incremental revenue. However, few (if any) of those canned promotions were conceived as part of a strategy for Branding.

In fact, even with genius operators like Johnny Winokur or genius marketers like Dennis Conrad, effective promotions are part of the Branding philosophy and are not in opposition to Branding; they are one of the building blocks of a Brand.

Promotions are to the casino as unloading those bricks is to the big picture of the overall construction project; a valuable, essential, tool.

Further complicated the model of building the Brand, getting to that "THE versus MY" level is not instant; it is a process that takes time. Usually, it is a multiple step process:

1. **Brand Recognition** is the first level of building that loyalty. A good example is that "California's Friendliest Casino," tag line that immediately makes me think of the Rolling Hills Casino. I recognize the Brand, though I know nothing else about it.
2. **Brand Awareness** is the next level toward the goal of loyalty. A good example can be seen in the Brand names "Cadillac", "Tiffany", or "Rolex". While you may not own any products of those Brands, you certainly are aware of them and their images. In fact, if I metaphorically say "it is the Cadillac of potatoes", you immediately know that I am talking about a top-of-the-line potato.
3. **Brand Loyalty** is that level of MY airline versus a generic THE airline. It is loyalty to such a degree that you would not even consider a competing Brand.

It is from this model that Brand value is built.

Sustainable Competitive Advantage

I cannot emphasize strongly enough the value that Branding brings to a property; yet sometimes it seems like a Brand is an abstract for which it is impossible to measure value.

Nonetheless, Branding is so key to out-performing competitors that it is essential for a business to find a consistent, reliable approach to understanding the customer-behavioral, the legal, and especially financial benefits of creating a great Brand.

Assigning a tangible valuation to that Brand, however, is not so easy. And at times I have found myself having to explain to Chief Financial Officers or Business Committees or Tribal Councils or Boards of Directors or to investors why I wanted to spend money on an intangible Brand.

Like with patents and copyrights, the intellectual property of a Brand is rarely listed on a corporate balance sheet (unless the company has been acquired by a third party that wants to show inflated value). Consequently, some of the world's most valuable Brands (like Apple, Google, etc.) add nothing to reported asset value on their balance sheets[3].

The biggest issue for putting a value on a Brand is that many analysts consider it an exercise of putting a dollar amount to "goodwill". That technique is a simple calculation of the enterprise value minus the value of the assets. Whatever number is left is the value of the "goodwill".

That method ignores revenue growth and actual multiples of EBITDA. Aware of this flaw, other analysts use a "pricing power" metric to assign value to a Brand.

---

[3] Stephen Johnson, *The Economist Guide to Intellectual Property* (London: Profile Books / Public Affairs / The Economist, 2015), 247.

For a traditional business, pricing power is a measure of how much extra can be charged for a Brand, based on its name. For example, how much more can General Mills charge for Cheerios than for Millville Crispy Oats, even though they are the exact same product owned by the same company? The difference is multiplied by the units sold and that determines how much the Brand is worth. In the casino version of that model, the price differential is determined by changing the hold of games ("tighter" slots). In the gaming industry, this is a really bad idea from a long-term planning standpoint.

There is an entire genre of businesses that do nothing but manage Brands for other companies. Because of the complexity of identifying a Brand's exact value, a number of these consultancies[4] have sprung up basing their business models on independently determining that value. Those companies then offer services to maximize that identified value through management of the client company's Brand to keep the value high.

While their specific methodologies differ, typically all use some variation of the *ISO 10668*[5] (International Organization for Standardization) specifications for the procedures and methods of measuring the value of a Brand. In that sense, then, Brand value becomes at

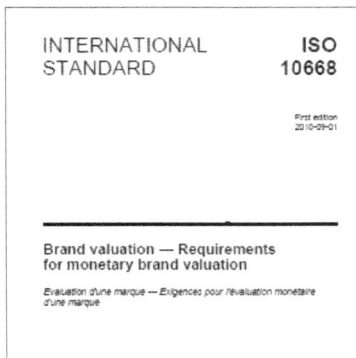

least somewhat tangible and there is actually an internationally-accepted procedure for determining Brand value.

---

[4] companies like Brand Finance, BrandZ, InterBrand (part of Omnicom), SuperBrands, CoolBrands, etc.,

[5] *"International Standard ISO 10668. With Brand valuation —Requirements for monetary Brand valuation"* (Geneva: International Organization for Standardization, 2010, v)

This is, at very least, a Godsend for marketers who have argued for years that their Branding efforts have "hard to define" benefits. With this model, those Benefits are no longer hard to define.

Those companies' most-widely-used model of "value-added theorems" was developed by Harvard Business School's Michael Porter and his "Sustainable Competitive Advantage" differentiators. His process conducts legal analyses, behavior analyses, and financial analyses to determine the impact of the Brand.

The companies then compare the combination of those techniques to the ISO 10668 guidelines. With that methodology, Brand value is immanently evident through a close look at either more business or market share increase after establishment of the Brand. This approach looks closely at the actual value generated by the Branding; value that is objectively transparent, reconcilable, and repeatable.

This determination easily can be made if we approach Branding in reverse —seemingly backward— by creating the Brand as a function of revenue rather than looking for revenue as a function of the Brand.

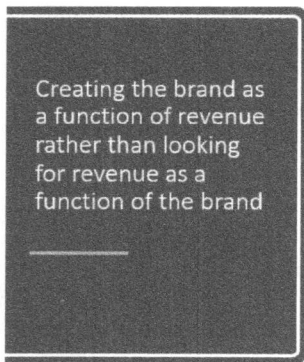

Creating the brand as a function of revenue rather than looking for revenue as a function of the brand

Branding

Branding

This double-talk-sounding technique puts you in control of both your Brand AND the revenue generated by your Brand. But to get to that point, you have to begin with a thorough understanding of how Brand promotion is generated.

Why Good Brands Go Bad

If Branding is THE magic bullet for success, then one has to wonder how some of the best-known Brands have succumbed to disastrous financial performance, bankruptcies, forced liquidation, or all three.

Some of the casino industry's most spectacular crashes have been in companies that had:

- Over-the-top Brand recognition;
- Finance-focused operators;
- Large, some publicly-traded, companies;
- What many would call "great" Brands (and I would say should-have-been-great)

These disasters have ruined or nearly-ruined some of what should have been the most successful casinos. Among the headline grabbers in the past few years:

- The financial calamities of Caesars (Harrah's) massive bankruptcy, resignation of their CEO, and subsequent seizure by corporate raider Carl Icahn;
- The revocation of the Tropicana gaming license in Atlantic City;
- The financial collapse of Donald Trump's casino empire;
- The shutdown of the Sahara in Vegas (and the SLS failings);
- Stations Casinos' Chapter 11 reorganization bankruptcy;
- The enormous failure of Colony's casino properties;
- The bankruptcy of Jerry's Nugget in North Las Vegas;
- The Federal investigation of Sheldon Adelson's Las Vegas Sands executives violating money-laundering laws;

- The revocation of Foxwoods' casino license in Pennsylvania.

Reasons (or excuses) for the failings are a litany of the "usual suspects":

- Failure to address the competition;
- Bad capital structures;
- Issues with the facilities or infrastructure;
- General failings of the economy;
- Under capitalization;
- Deception or theft;
- Miscalculations of the market;
- And on and on...

Even some of the strongest-Brand operators found themselves unfocused on their core business of gambling and enmeshed in CMBS and RMBS (commercial mortgage-backed securities and residential mortgage-backed securities) as integral to their financing (and we all know what happened to the mortgage backed securities world).

Like that cavalier dabbling in financial derivatives, in almost every case, in reality the most spectacular failings have come from focusing resources in something other than the core Brand.

The most common actual reasons for the majority of failings (regardless of the excuses) are:

1. Focusing resources on areas other than the core business and the established Brand;
2. Having no real Brand identity to serve as a market differentiator;
3. Or, in Indian Country, mistaking Tribal identity for a gambling Brand.

Any of these common mistakes can be detrimental to success.

Equally detrimental, failure to constantly maintain and service the Brand can be a stake-through-the-heart of a once healthy Brand; more on this failing later.

Part 2: Projecting Earnings

It Is Not Experiment-driven

Only a few casino operators would list their Brand as a valuable business asset. Fewer would consider it an active marketing tool (as opposed to a passive byproduct of marketing). And, most financial operators would never include Brand Exploitation in their toolbox for projecting financial performance, cost control, or revenue generation.

Yet, when correctly executed a great Brand generates financial results —earnings, EBITDA— that can be projected with a high degree of accuracy and reliability; more so than probably any other methodology

Delta did not give me all of that extra service because I am famous. They didn't do it because I am the star of a television show nor because I am a best-selling author. They didn't do it because I lecture on Branding and they wanted a good review. They didn't even do it because they hoped I would tell all of my friends what a swell airline Delta is. Nope.

In fact, Delta didn't know me from anyone else. What they DID know was that one of their computer algorithms generated an alert that a Diamond Frequent Flyer would be arriving with an impossibly tight schedule. That triggered a specific protocol and series of events that resulted in printing the little sign and sending the agent to meet me at the arriving flight.

Think about that! Delta flies 4,804 flights every day with something like 193-million passengers annually. They have more than 81-million members in their frequent-flyer program and more than 60,000 Diamond members. At best, I am just a frequent-flyer number to them; But to ME… Delta is MY airline.

25

I was paying an average of $600 per flight; multiplied by at least 150 flights annually, I was paying Delta airlines at least $90,000 a year. If I had used discount carriers and ticket-bidding web sites, I probably could have flown for half that (or less). So, I was paying Delta a premium of at least $45,000 a year; and who knows what their actual cost would have been to fly that first-class seat empty —certainly, nothing near the $600 that I was paying.

Delta has no additional overhead costs of personal hosts or representatives assigned to even the best customers, like me; everything they did was a completely automated computer process until they dispatched the drivers. As a company, Delta Airlines and its employees had no idea of the particulars of any individual customer; but, again, on that personal level, Delta was MY airline.

They were not only my preferred airline, but they were the only airline that gave me all those perks.

What a magnificent marketing coup! They created a personal relationship between the company and the individual... without ever having known the individual.

Effective Branding Begins With A
PLAN

It was all about my perception. A carefully crafted perception; it was all part of a complex plan. Delta planned and calculated my perception and even accurately projected revenue based on my perception.

They didn't guess, they didn't experiment, they didn't do any of it because it was "cool". It was all part of a calculated plan to assure that I continued to spend $90,000 a year —or more— with them. And... it worked.

What if we could do that for a casino (or any other business)? What if a player refused to go to a competing casino because they loved our casino so much? Again, what a magnificent marketing coup!

Financial results can be projected with a high degree of accuracy and reliability. Unlike the top-secret formulas for Coca-Cola, Bush's Baked Beans, Dr. Pepper, McDonald's special sauce, Famous Amos Cookies, or the Colonel's KFC recipe these formulas are widely available and easy to follow.

The "magic formulas" for creating this level of predictability and profit comes from a group of systems proven in multiple industries and their verticals:

- Almost a half-century ago, Texas Instruments created their "zero-based budgeting" system merging the budging process with top-level strategic objectives; a system adopted by governments, other corporations, and even entire industries.

- For almost as long, the direct marketing cataloging industry[6] has relied on a customer-tracking methodology that has repeatedly provided accurate projections; a system in use today by Amazon and other major retailers.

- Since the golden age of Las Vegas, operators there repeatedly have been pronounced dead as customer markets changed. Each time they defied the pundits and bounced back; using these formulaic techniques.

No matter how complex, flashy, or crowd-enticing a promotion may be or how strong the underlying Branding appears to the customer, beneath the surface of the successful ones is always a fixed analysis with calculated projections.

---

[6] (https://thedma.org/)

Revenue Sources

In order to position a Brand to generate maximum revenue and accurately project that revenue, we first need to be perfectly clear about the sources of that income: what drives it.

Determining the sources of revenue is necessary, regardless of the industry, because Brand decisions need to be tied to hard data and not to speculation.

The process begins, complexly, with identifying the current source(s) of the majority of our revenue. As simple as that sounds, too-often it is a complicated maze to define the difference between the income from business <u>units</u> and <u>sources</u>.

Business units typically include:

- Casino;
- Hotel;
- F&B (restaurants and bars, sometimes separated for accounting purposes);
- Entertainment;
- Retail;
- ...and other units

Sources of the revenue —why the customers decided to spend in each business unit— can include:

- Walk-in business;
- Lack of competition in the area, making the property the only option;
- Specific promotions or offers;
- Advertising;
- Direct mail;
- ... or the BRAND.

That seems like a simple differentiation but making it complex is often used to obfuscate uncertain business models from skittish investors or wary Tribal Councils.

For example, in the casino industry, a number of operators have argued in interviews, during investor conference calls, and to trade associations, that gambling —as a business unit— provides only a small portion of corporate revenue.

Despite widespread media reports that gaming is no longer the primary revenue source for casino-hotel-resort Brands, the facts tell a different story. Nationwide, gambling revenue —predominantly slot machine revenue— makes up 80% of the income for casino-hotel-resorts. Even among the world's mega-operators, these numbers hold true.

COMPANY	PERCENTAGE OF REVENUE FROM GAMBLING	
Melco Crown	94.8%	
Pinnacle	89.4%	
Penn National	88%	*Less than 14% of revenue from Las Vegas*
Boyd Gaming	84%	
LV Sands	79%	
Wynn	71.9%	
Caesars	63.6%*	*majority of revenue from Las Vegas*
MGM	48.7%*	

Only in Las Vegas does this deviate; primarily because Las Vegas properties have changed their business models to a convention business catering to once-a-year visitors rather than multiple-times-a-week guests. And even in Las Vegas, the gaming revenue is still significantly higher than most undocumented reports.

Most notoriously, *The Economist* magazine reported that Las Vegas Venetian[7] owner Sheldon Adelson claim that he is not in the gambling business and that 70% of his revenue comes from non-gaming revenue centers. The magazine further reported:

"Mr. Adelson, the head of Las Vegas Sands and for some years the world's third-richest person, insists that he is not in the gambling business, nor even in the gaming business (a distinction he and Michael Leven, Las Vegas Sands' president, consider important; the difference between gaming and gambling, according to Mr. Leven, "is the difference between having a cocktail and going out drinking")."[8]

---

[7] on the NYSE as LVS; Las Vegas Sands
[8] http://www.economist.com/node/16507768?story_id=16507768&fsrc=rss

Despite that lofty distancing from the not-so-pretty history of the gambling business, a review of their annual reports reveals that actually 79% of their revenue comes from gambling. More specifically, Investopedia reports:

> *"For every dollar Las Vegas Sands takes in from room fees — and remember, the company has 7,000 rooms at one joint property alone — it takes in $8.24 in gambling revenue. Dining, shopping, and convention revenue combined barely match the money garnered by renting out rooms.[9]"*

Understand what that means! Their casinos make more than eight-times what their "non-gaming" businesses make.

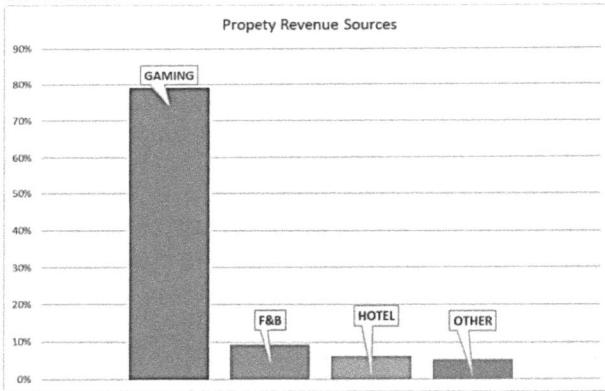

Propety Revenue Sources

It is empirically correct that despite reports or corporate claims, an average of 80% of property revenue (excluding on the Las Vegas strip) comes from gambling.

---

[9] https://www.investopedia.com/articles/markets/041715/how-las-vegas-sands-lvs-makes-its-money.asp

Transforming a Brand to Revenue

One of the many ways the casino model differs from most other industries is that we have one business unit that generates 80% of our revenue. This gives us a fast-track opportunity for transforming a Brand into a revenue machine.

The model and formulas we will explore work for any multi-business-unit industry where any one or two units generate more than half of the revenue.

Clearly then, the first step in the process is to identfy the business unit(s) that out-performs others. For our industry, it is the casino. Knowing that gives us a starting point to explore transformative formulas that change a *merely-a-label* Brand into a powerful revenue machine.

The next step is to create that Delta-Airlines-style loyalty and then create a process that translates that loyalty to predictable, trackable, and significant revenue.

That begins by understanding and applying the sales-science behind that large retail chain's back-of-the-house red-lights paradigm.

These processes require the collection, analysis, and acting on data. That data becomes the nuts-and-bolts of projecting, generating, and controlling day-to-day revenue. The most "radical" concept that I am presenting here is that the Brand is THE driving force for revenue. THAT is the takeaway from all of this.

With this technique, the Brand becomes much more than an addition to market cap, earnings multipliers, or book value. The Brand and management of the Brand become the single largest source of revenue.

Almost all business schools will teach that a Brand gives added value to a business; but in the real world, the Brand is much more than a corporate finance tool for inflating valuation of a business and impressing investors or Tribal Councils.

Creating Economies of Scale

L et's make some logical assumptions based on the actual reported tax-reported numbers rather than sensationalist claims or corporate misdirection:

1. Based on measurable taxation data and other public reporting, we know that nationwide an average of 80% of casino-resort-hotel revenue comes from the casino business unit and specifically from slots.

2. We know that for a well-run business —in almost any industry— it should cost something less than 80% of its revenue to operate the business; that is, to pay all operating expenses.

Therefore:

All revenue from non-gaming amenities (hotel, F&B, entertainment, etc.) can go directly to the bottom line. In this model it could cost NOTHING to operate those amenities; their costs are paid 100% by gaming revenue.

From the number of paperclips needed to the number of hours a slot attendant is needed to how much food the restaurant needs in stock to how much paper is needed to print TITO tickets: every line-item expense can vary based on the volume of business.

If you could control that volume of business, you could control operating expenses.

It is a very simple concept. In fact, it is a modification of the aforementioned 1970's-era "decision packages" of the Texas Instruments model called "zero-based budgeting" (ZBB). The often-proven system has been adopted by companies across multiple industries (Heinz, Kraft Foods, Oracle Software, and others) as well as by government agencies.

To implement the system, there are two steps:

a) determine the ratio of cost-to-revenue of each line item; and

b) build a budget "backwards" basing each line item on the volume of business; the amount of revenue.

To get a good handle on those line-item-by-line-item ratios, there are a number of excellent sources for data comparison and benchmarking:

- Nevada Gaming Control publishes an annual Nevada Gaming Abstract, with category (though not line-item) expense to income ratios;

- That report makes a great companion to the Risk Management Association's "Hotel / Casinos, Credit Considerations" report.

- Several gaming states publish similar casino reports that, when poured over, can help shape expected fixed ratios of operating costs. Other states, like New Jersey for example, don't publish a Nevada-like abstract, but they do provide the raw data as a matter of public record.

- Several casino auditing firms also make generic casino comparisons available.

- I have always liked the annual "Cost of Doing Business" report from Joseph Eve (Wipfli) which provides departmental-level breakdowns based on the revenue-size of Tribal casinos.

- Casino City Press publishes the very-well researched "Indian Gaming Industry Report" from Dr. Alan Meister.

Line-item variances shown in most of these reports are actual numbers according to casino size, revenue, and competitive factors.

Even Goldman-Sachs acknowledges this methodology; they project maintenance costs, for example, at 10% to 15% of property revenue and they recognize that marketing and promotional expenses can vary as well.

My own company combines a "best of breed" synthesis of several of these benchmarks and pairs them with our own proprietary figures. Using this technique, we are able to determine how much of that 80%-of-property-revenue (from slots) it takes to operate the entire property.

From that exercise, we are able to fulfill the second step of that equation: building a budget "backwards" basing each line item on the volume of business; the amount of revenue.

The only issue remaining, then, is to manage the operation so that it fits into the budgeting parameters we create.

These ZBB formulas apply to any business unit that has such lopsided revenue performance. In any unit that accounts for 55% or more of total property revenue, then all revenue from the amenity business units can go directly to the bottom line. Again, in this model it cost NOTHING to operate those amenities, because their costs are paid 100% by revenue from the dominant unit.

Whether the source of customers comes from walk-ins, targeted direct mail, advertising, a lack of competition, specific offers, or other sources... the one consistent thread is the Brand.

In the available management and marketing arsenal, management of the Brand is the only consistently successful tool to focus on, track, and increase revenue.

Other techniques inevitably lead to failure; often times disastrously imploding despite indications that all is well.

Part 3: Increase & Track Revenue

20 Questions Toward Branding

Whether you are selling Cheerios (or Millville Crispy Oats) or lawn mowers or hotel rooms or time-in-chair at a slot machine, the "Marketing 101" rule for generating more revenue is the same: "find out who your best customers are and then go get a lot more just like them."

That proposition is often easier said than done. It can be a lot like Alice's encounter with the Cheshire cat. Overwhelmed with Wonderland, she asked the cat, "Would you tell me, please Sir, which way I ought to go from here? Oh my, where to begin?" The wily old cat just grinned and then finally advised the young girl, "At the beginning, my dear." Like the cool cat's advice to the Wonderland visitor, we need to know where to begin.

For the casino world, that is DATA. The SINGLE most important factor in beginning Branding revenue is determine your Brand's target. Once we fully understand the target, only then can we *assure* revenue from a Brand.

We start the process by reviewing our customer database from the player-tracking system. As recently as 15-years-ago, this was not an easy process:

- Many properties didn't have player tracking systems at all;
- Most of those that did have systems did not segment their players by tiers of value to the casino;
- Most that had systems did not have the capability of interfacing with their hotel systems or their POS systems;
- Most that had systems did not have multi-property interoperability;

- In Class II electronic-bingo properties many of the game vendors refused to allow third-party systems to touch their data or allow their data to be in the same system as competitor's data.

In some areas it still is not as simple as it sounds and has not improved much in the past decade and a half:

- Most systems require the purchase of costly special modules to obtain even the most-essential functions;
- Without third-party plug-ins or even more expensive modules, many systems require a costly in-house staff of data analysts and technicians to be able to fully use the data;
- Even with in-house staff, some properties still have to export their data to an external company to analyze it then sort it for direct-mail and other uses;
- In most cases, marketing analysts have to create offers/promotions.

There are very few systems that provide all of this functionality out-of-the-box (without buying modules, add-ons, and hiring experts).

Nonetheless, if we know the right questions to ask, it is relatively simple to pull the data we need to start shaping the Brand to enhance revenue. We start that process by reviewing the customer database from the player-tracking system. The first step is to divide that database into segments or tiers of similar customers.

Most of us already use tier-levels that allow us to target different promotions to different customer types. But for the sake of understanding how we are going to use those standard marketing tools for Brand enhancement, let's go through some simple exercises to help us better understand how to use our segmented data.

INITIAL SETUP OF TIERS

We CAN start by summarizing all players into one of four key-worth criteria:

1. $500+ Average Daily Theoretical (ADT)
2. $100 - $499.99

3. $25 - $99.99
4. $0 - $24.99

Using "actual" rather than theoretical (theo) gives a much more micro-accurate analysis of the customer base; however, for the first take on how tiers work, we will use the more common measure: ADT. The initial data categories, then, look like this:

ENTIRE CUSTOMER BASE
- total # of customers
- total gaming revenue

| $500+ | $100-$499 | $25-$99 | $0-$24.99 |

A micro-accurate targeting might use more than four segments; but, again, for the initial targeting we will use these four common segments. Once the system is in place, this can be fine-tuned later.

Within each of these monetary value "buckets", we next analyze the customer base by geography. Starting with a map of the casino location, draw a circle encompassing 30 miles, a second circle encompassing 60 miles, and additional concentric circles at 90 miles, and 120 miles. In the next step we will determine which players in each monetary bucket fit into which circles. Doing this, we will inevitably find that some of addresses will be unreadable or invalid; even those should be tracked.

CONCENTRIC CIRCLE		Distance from Casino
Inner Circle		Within 30 miles
Middle Circle		31 to 60 miles
Outer Circle		61 to 90 miles
Extended Circle		91 to 120 miles
Not plotted	•	Beyond 120 miles
	•	Invalid addresses

Eventually, and again for micro-targeting purposes, we might later subdivide each of these circles into smaller circles, zip-codes, or even streets. But, for the purposes here, we will start with these five geographic segments.

Next, we will populate the four geographic (and one invalid) segments with the following data:
- Total number of customers inside each circle;
- Percentage of total customer base in each circle; and
- Total revenue (casino win) within each circle.

Each monetary segment then will look like this example:

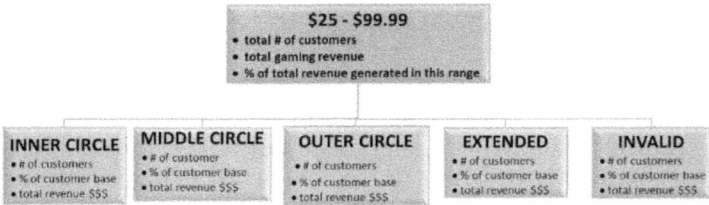

$25 - $99.99
• total # of customers
• total gaming revenue
• % of total revenue generated in this range

INNER CIRCLE	MIDDLE CIRCLE	OUTER CIRCLE	EXTENDED	INVALID
• # of customers	• # of customer	• # of customers	• # of customers	• # of customers
• % of customer base	• % of customer base	• % of customer base	• % of customer base	• % of customer base
• total revenue $$$	• total revenue $$$	• total revenue $$$	• total revenue $$$	• total revenue $$$

Next, divide each geographic circle into categories:
1. Predominately Slot Players; and
2. Predominately Other Games (Tables, Bingo, etc.).

Then populate each of those categories with the same data we used to populate each circle:
- Total number of customers in each category;
- Percentage of total customer base in each category;
- Total revenue (casino win) in each category;
- … and a 4th level:
- The percentage of each circle's market that is either slot or other game.

Each circle, then, will have this data:

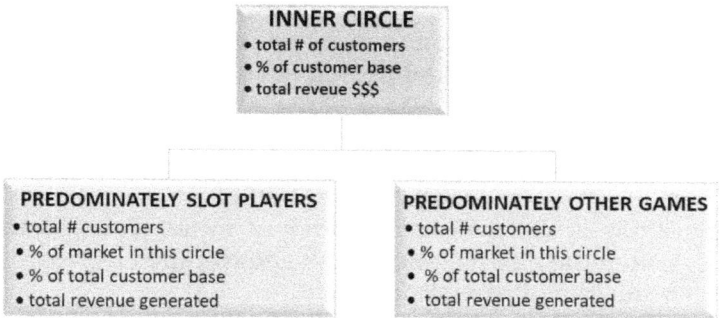

```
                    INNER CIRCLE
                 • total # of customers
                 • % of customer base
                 • total reveue $$$
```

```
PREDOMINATELY SLOT PLAYERS        PREDOMINATELY OTHER GAMES
 • total # customers               • total # customers
 • % of market in this circle      • % of market in this circle
 • % of total customer base        • % of total customer base
 • total revenue generated         • total revenue generated
```

    With the addition of these data points, the structure of each monetary bucket should look like this:

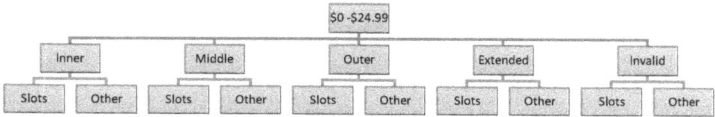

```
                              $0 -$24.99
      Inner        Middle        Outer       Extended      Invalid
   Slots  Other  Slots  Other  Slots  Other  Slots  Other  Slots  Other
```

This chart above represents one monetary tier only. The overall database is divided into four monetary segments, in this example. Each of those segments needs to be divided into the five geographic segments. And, each of those five geo-segments is further divided into either slot or games segments. In short, that gives us 10 segments per monetary bucket or 40 segments total, for this model.

    Now that we have the data segmented, let's play "Twenty Questions". These are 20 common questions that we need to know about our customers before we begin to use our segmentation:

OVERVIEW QUESTIONS:

1. What percentage of total game-play is tracked? (Meaning, what percentage of all players are using their cards?) This metric should be a central focus for any marketing campaign because the more play that is tracked the more accurate our campaigns will be.

2. During the period tracked (week, month, quarter, year, etc.) how much total theoretical (or actual) win was generated for the casino?

3. What was the average win per day per guest?
4. What was the average number of days played per customer per tracked period (week, month, quarter, year, etc.)?
5. How many visits did the average customer make to the casino?

ABOUT OUR MARKET

6. What is the average number of miles traveled to reach the casino (and which geographic circle provides the most visitors)?
7. What is the average number of miles traveled from within each circle?
8. How many (and what percentage of) players reside in the inner-most market (circle)?
9. What is the average daily theo (theoretical casino win) from players in each circle?
10. What is the average number of days played by people in each circle?

GAMES & TYPES OF PLAY

11. What percentage of players played slots predominantly and what percentage of overall Average Daily Theoretical (casino win) did they generate?
12. What is the Average Daily Theoretical ("ADT") of slot players and the ADT of other games players?
13. What is the average number of days played in the period by slot players and by players of other games?

WORTH

14. What percentage of the database had ADT in each of the defined monetary categories?
15. What is the correlation between ADT and number of days played?
16. What percentage of the database falls into each monetary category?

LIFE CYCLE

Typically, a customer's "lifecycle" for a casino flows into four phases: (1) Acquisition; (2) Retention; (3) Defection; and (4) Reactivation.

17. What percentage of tracked players are new players for this time period?

18. What percentage of players defected between the last two measured periods of time?
19. What percentage of players are reactivated after going for at least one measured period of no activity?
20. What percentage of players showed no change in their lifecycle of play?

These twenty questions now need to be repeated for each sub-segment:

- for Predominately Slots Players within each monetary bucket; and
- for Predominantly Other Games Players within each monetary bucket.

Starting with this basic understanding of our customers base, we are now going to segment those customers into a precision targeting system.

Standard customer-targeting models usually measure customer behavior with demographics, geography, and choice of product... all weighed against the *monetary value of visits*. This is what we did above with the "20 Questions" from the data.

That technique of data-marketing is very effective for *some* industries; and it *does* give a basis for creating promotions that drive casino traffic. Using geographic data, basic census data, demographic data, and basic behavior data allows us to create those very general offers.

With that level of targeting, groups of customers are shot-gunned with a barrage of offers that may or may not hit the mark. There are, of course, many ways to fine-tune that targeting; age, gender, education level, specific game preferences, lead scores, sales funnel stage, customer personae and many more.

There are some very-few marketers who from experience can almost-instinctively do the 20-Questions analysis without running the data. Those savants are few and far between and we do not recommend trying to emulate them.

Regardless of how fine-tuned those methods may be, what they do NOT provide is trackable, verifiable, underline-grade projections of revenue. Moreover, they do not give us the insights as to who, specifically by name, our most valuable customers are, who needs nurturing, and who deserves our most lucrative offers.

To accomplish those goals, we need a precision-focused technique; creating highly-specialized offers tailored personally (or seemingly so) for each individual customer and potential customer. We need a methodology of touching the customer-player individually and directly. We need to direct-market.

The most successful direct marketers in the history of the world were the pre-internet paper-catalog companies; with the internet, Amazon has led the way in applying those techniques to the modern epoch.

In this model, a cataloguer, like *L.L. Bean* for example, produced a nice paper catalog which they mailed out all over America; millions of copies. An average catalog was between 50 and 250 pages of their merchandise which was useful all over the country. The key to sales was getting the customers to flip through all those pages; and that was done with the front cover of the catalog... the *offer*.

The creative process includes determining what to put on that front cover that will cause potential customers to open it and look at the merchandise. In a winter catalog, customers in Montana (for example) may be really excited about heavy coats, snow boots, and other cold-winter gear, or a simple snowy mountain scene; but in South Florida, where the temperature in February is 80-degrees, the snowbound catalog isn't going to excite locals to open it (though the pages inside are identical).

To solve that targeting problem, catalog companies sent different front covers to different constituencies; in this example, based on geographic location. That is similar to our first analysis for our "twenty questions".

If the company goes to all the trouble to create different versions of the cover based on zip codes, then there are other common factors they can add in by using other data. For example, to encourage a past customer to reorder, the company might offer a 10% discount for returning customers; and that offer may be printed in huge red letters on the front of the catalog sent to only returning customers. That customer's next-door neighbor may have never ordered from the company; so, the enticement offer might be "free shipping for new customers" printed in bright colors on the front of the catalog. Different covers — even next door to each other.

Using this method, catalog companies were able to target customers on multi-dimensional levels. That meant having an entire selection of different covers for that winter catalog.

Just in this example, they had the northern and southern versions and within those versions they have regular customers and not-so-regular customers. Just in that simple example there are four different covers for that winter catalog. Every customer for their company could be grouped into one of those categories.

Get it? The offer appears to be personal to the customer; but in reality, it is merely using the data to group types of customers to types of offers most likely to elicit a response. Thousands of "like" customers received the same "personalized" offer.

Transpose that incredibly successful model to our casinos, and we can turn loose the creative juices to devise all sorts of specialized offers based on types of games played, frequency of visits to the casino, how far they had to come to get to our casino, how much they typically gamble, and any other creative combination we can devise.

The more precision the segmentation of the data, the more likely the customer is to act on the offer.

THE TAKEAWAY: Application of the data from these 20 Questions routinely increases casino revenue double-digit compared to not using the data this way. It is a long-proven multiple-industry technique of customer engagement. It is, as that Cheshire Cat directed, the beginning.

43

The Secret of RFM

For several years the buzz-words around casino marketing have been "CRM" (customer relationship management); "the customer journey"; "actionable analytics"; and a specialized targeting term, "RFM" (recency, frequency, and monetary value).

Other than lofty-sounding acronyms, in reality most casino marketers either rely on whatever modules the player tracking system provides; or they just banter around the terms without really applying them.

Nonetheless, RFM is the single most important tool for shaping Brand value.

These are essential elements that can be used for personalized targeting to fill slot machine seats on a day-to-day basis and build the kind of tangible loyalty that Delta built with me.

Once we understand how to construct the RFM targeting model, we can examine how to convert that model to daily casino revenue and tie it to the Branding.

"R" = Recency

This is when a player last gambled in a casino. The knowledge of how recently a customer gambled gives us the beginning ability to project the value that customer has (to us or to other casinos, if we chose to sell that customer's name).

It does not reveal, however, if this is a repeat customer; an important factor in venues where competition is high.

"F" = Frequency.

This is how often a player comes in. We should be able to measure the frequency of casino play as either one-time visitors or as repeat players. (This can also factor in hands-per -hour at tables or (more likely) handle-pulls (or button pushes) per quarter-hour of slot play).

However, this measure does not identify the last time the player visited the casino. They may have played five times last year; or once a month for five months; we need the above "recency" for that measure.

"M" = Monetary Value

This is how much money a player gambles. (Net revenue from that gambling is a mathematical function of the hold; so, the ADT (Average Daily Theoretical) or ADA (Average Daily Actual) are merely calculations from how much a customer plays.)

Modeling

To build our targeting model, we will begin with the "R" — recency. Let's start with a simplified chart of repeat customer activity that looks like the chart below:

Played Today					
Played With A Week					
Within 30 Days					
This Quarter					
This Year					

If we consider a top axis to add the "F" of RFM (Frequency), then we should be able to put together a full graphic analysis of two dimensions of our customers. (For the purpose of this basic illustration, we will exclude the plays-per-hour portion of the Frequency plotting ... though in real application of this technique it is an essential element for accurate projections).

	Played 5 or more times	Played 4 or more times	Played 3 or more times	Played Twice	Played Once
Played Today					
Played With A Week					
Within 30 Days					
This Quarter					
This Year					

Having established two axes for customer plotting, let's identify each of the positions where we should be able to enter data to plot customer behavior. In each block we should be able to insert the number of (or the names of) customers who match the criteria for that block.

To simplify this example, we are only including 25 possible plotting positions for our customers; in reality that number (at least for our proprietary methodology) would be a minimum of 80 to 120, depending on the total size of the database (and could be as high as 1,000+ segments). To visualize the plotting for this example, we will identify each block with a letter of the alphabet.

	Played 5 or more times	Played 4 or more times	Played 3 or more times	Played Twice	Played Once
Played Today	A	B	C	D	E
Played With A Week	F	G	H	I	J
Within 30 Days	K	L	M	N	O
This Quarter	P	Q	R	S	T
This Year	U	V	W	X	Y

In this example above, customers in block A played 5 times (or more) and played one of those times today. Likewise, customers in Block F played 5 times and one of those times was this week but not today. Continuing the plotting, customers in Block Y played once last year. Customers in block U played 5 times, but not in the past year...and so on.

This example-charting allows us to examine the behavior of our best customers...either by number or by name (thanks to database technology). This within itself is a powerful tool because it allows us immediately to tailor different offers to different customers, based on this little bit of data.

In short, we can contact those customers (for example) in Block U who spent money with us five times but not recently. We can launch a marketing campaign to (1) determine why they have not been back, and (2) create an offer to entice them to come back.

Again, for the purpose of simplification in understanding the processes here, let's merge some of these blocks into quadrants so that we can easily see our best customers, our worst customers, and our borderline customers.

Even though we are using simple charts here, remember that in reality a computer is keeping track of all of this data for us and sorting the players into our categories. In reality, these seemingly time-consuming and expensive models are instant and virtually cost free.

	5 or more	4 or more	3 or more	Played Twice	Played Once
Played Today			C		
Played With A Week	A, B, F, G, K, L		H	D, E, I, J, N, O	
Within 30 Days			M		
This Quarter	P, Q, U, V		R	S, T, X, Y	
This Year			W		

Customers in grid ABFGKL are our best customers; while customers in grid STXY are our worst customers (in relative terms, of course). The other grids have varying values to us as good or bad customers.

Now if we also modify our axis to match our grids, we get a simplified chart that looks like this:

	4 or more times	3 or more	Once or Twice
Played Today to 30 days ago	A, B, F, G, K, L	C H M	D, E, I, J, N, O
This Quarter to one year ago	P, Q, U, V	R W	S, T, X, Y

This over simplification very easily shows us how we, conceptually, should be able to rank customers based on "R" (recency) and "F" (frequency) data. We can also see how easy it is to start targeting specific offers to customers based on their behavior (and therefore to what they are most like to respond).

This model holds true, unless we consider the possibility that each of the customers in grid ABFGKL played one credit on penny slots while the customers in grid STXY each played maximum credits on $5 slots; then suddenly our two-dimensional graph is seriously skewed in any plan to use it to measure "good customers".

And it is herein that a lot of segmentation fails in its striving for accuracy; stopping at this point in segmentation is a serious failure except in the hands of the aforementioned savant-like operators and marketers who can analyze players seemingly intuitively.

Two-dimensional segmenting just falls short. Fortunately, the Greek philosopher and mathematician Euclid taught us that the world is not two-dimensional. Equally fortunately, neither is the understanding of customer history. The third dimension for us is that "M" —Monetary Value.

That is where, in part, we started the data analytics process. We now have analyzed two of the RFM dimensions: "R" and "F". In the context of RFM, let's first consider a standalone chart of the previously analyzed monetary value of customers. We will chart average bets placed in our four per-session categories: $0 to $24.99, $25 to $99, $100 to $499, and $500+ ADT (or actual). This will be our left axis. The top axis, then, is a little more complex.

If we rate the customers as "big spender", "average spender", and "worse spender", then the task will be to determine what steps we must take in each category to increase a lower player to become a bigger spender; and more importantly to create the next-level of loyalty. The top axis then is the category of spending:

	Big Spender	Average Spender	Worse Spender
$500+	A		
$100-$499		B	
$25-$99			C
$0-$24.99			

In the A block, all the players are already spending in our top (over simplified, for this example) segment, so no movement is necessary; however, retention IS a major issue. In the B block, players must be retained AND move one level to become our best spending players. And in the C block the customers must be retained and move two levels to become best...and move one level even to become average.

The Big Spender category, then, should receive the most attention in attempting to retain them, to get them to play more times and more often. The ones who spend almost nothing should have fewer resources dedicated to moving them toward spending more often and more times. This is one of many possible basic marketing strategies that most good marketers already deal with on a daily basis.

NOW...If we superimpose this model onto our "R" and "F" chart from above, we should be able to quickly see that a player who spends the most AND has recently played and plays often is our very best customer.

Likewise, the player who spends the least, has only played once, and has not played in the past year...is the worst customer. Everyone else falls somewhere between in a (vastly over simplified) three-dimensional graph of this RFM data.

This gives us a three-dimensional matrix for our data analysis. To keep it simple for illustrative purposes, we can combine categories; but in the computer-generated version the matrix will be huge. The simplified 3-D matrix looks like this:

$501-$1000 / $100-$500 / $1-$100	Big Spender / Average Spender / Worse Spender		
	Played 4 times or more	Played 3 times	Played once or twice
Played Today to 30 days ago	A, B, F, G, K, L	C H M R W	D, E, I, J, N, O
Played this Quarter to one year ago	P, Q, U, V		S, T, X, Y

Of course, this table is vastly simplistic (created only for example); however, it does illustrate one general technique of how we market our casino once we have a player history.

THE TAKEAWAY: With this method of sorting player data, we have a powerful personalization tool to add to our already-existing arsenal of explicit user ratings, observed behavior, and demographic/psychographic information: we can create a highly-targeted offer based on this RFM table.

Even the best player tracking systems and their expensive data-mining software cousins, rarely use a full RFM table. Creating those offers, personalized with all the bells and whistles associated with suggestive selling, is a monstrously complex process but, it is a process well worth the effort; and it can be further fine-tuned.

The fun begins now!

Part 4: Changing markets
Setting Data-Driven Activity

These segmentation techniques provide the most effective foundation for what I earlier described as "Marketing 101"; find out who your best customers are and go get a lot more just like them.

The RFM-based marketing methodology is a specialized and very intense system that repeatedly has increased casino revenues by a minimum of 40% over pre-implementation. It has never failed to provide at least that much increase.

While as a marketing strategy it is essential to our Branding, it does not provide the Branding itself. Using my Delta example, it would be as if Delta had all of that data about my spending, my frequency, and my activity but did nothing with it. It would be as if they never dispatched that Porsche, ignored my "Diamond" status when I flew, and just included me in the pool of regular customers; maybe offering me an occasional discounted fare.

With the existing information, we can create pro-forma income data, balance sheet data, and cash flows analyses <u>tied to each individual customer</u>.

While this is great for promotions, service, and offers (like the Delta experience), the process of converting marketing to a Brand requires a little more data. Once the additional information is matched with our targeting matrices, the transformation can begin.

The amalgamation (not extrapolation) of that data defines micro-analytics of marketing management.

A subsequent application of all that collected data (including the additional information) to both a strategic plan and to a pro-forma forecast gives us the basis to craft our Brand. That newly-crafted Branding then has built into it the tools to be a **revenue machine!**

Henny Penny, Chicken Little, Baby Boomers, and Millennials

The Brothers Grimm published an 1823 story of Henny Penny; a hysterical chicken who mistakenly believed that the sky was falling and disaster was imminent. The story was written as a fabled warning not to believe everything one is told.

In the USA we know the story as Chicken Little; in the casino world I call the story "the Millennials are coming".

My version of the story has casino marketers determining that the "best-customer" profile identified by data analyses might not be still the best customer in ten years. That leads to anxiety over how to change a worse-customer demographic to replace the current best-customer demographic (without hurting the current customer base).

Fueled by widespread media reports and game vendors wanting to sell new types of games, scores of marketers, operators, and business committees have predicted "the falling sky" of the aging of the Baby Boomer generation and the rise of the Millennial generation.

My favorite purveyance of the pending doom can from a national magazine that wrote:

Vegas — Is Boom Overextended?

"A new breed of visitor is showing up (in Vegas) … to enjoy the good rooms, food, and shows but —and this is where it hurts— not to gamble."

"This new generation, the largest in the history of the world, clearly doesn't have their parents' and grandparents' propensity for gambling. Now there is major international pop-culture media announcing that these kids are more interested in bars, music, and entertainment. A generation raised in the high-tech world of gadgetry could not have the attention span to gamble like their greyed elders."

These journalistic pundits went on to list all the reasons that the gambling industry would collapse when

the older generation dies out and the younger generation takes their places in society:
- They are the single largest generation in the history of the world;
- They don't gamble;
- The have low net worth;
- The spend disposable income on bars, music, and entertainment;
- They dominate consumer spending across all sectors;
- They are driven by technology and stare at screens in all their spare time;
- They have short attention spans;
- They seek adventure;
- They find slot machine boring.

I have to admit, that is a pretty accurate assessment of passing the torch to the next generation; and it paints a pretty bleak picture for the future of the industry. Clearly, if our industry is to survive, we need to know all we can about that new generation of consumers.

If we are going to build a Brand that generates revenue, then we need to fully understand our target market.

The only problem is this seemingly perfectly on-target market assessment came from the June 20, 1955 issue of **LIFE MAGAZINE**. It was an article predicting the doom of the casino industry because the "new generation" of BABY BOOMERS weren't gamblers like their parents of "The Greatest Generation".

LAS VEGAS—IS BOOM OVEREXTENDED?
THE WAR ON VIRUS DISEASES
ROBERT GUGGENHEIM TELLS OF SAUDS NEW GOALS

NEWEST IN LAS VEGAS:
GIRLS AT THE MOULIN ROUGE

JUNE 20, 1955

Panic vs. Data

Branding MUST be based on data and not on spec-ulation. The truth is that despite feelings, instinct, reports, fears, or even observation, the best measure is always data; information.

Since the Millennial issue is of such pressing Branding and marketing focus, let's see what we actually know and how what we know impacts the Branding plan. We can start with Life Magazine's points and contrast the Millennials with the Baby Boomers.

	BABY BOOMERS	MILLENNIALS
They don't Gamble; low net worth	👍	👍
Spending on bars, music, & entertainment	👍	👍
Largest segment of population	👍	👍
They dominate consumer spending	👍	👍
Spend at high-end trendy restaurants	👍	👍
Driven by technology *(TV in 60's/ Internet cell 2018)*	👍	👍
Short attention span	👍	👍
Seek adventure; slots machines are boring	👍	👍
	end of casinos	*end of casinos*

There is a tremendous amount of data available for such a comparison/contrast; but in reality, it boils down to this:

- There are fewer millennials than "Generation X"; but more than Boomers. So why the panic?
- Millennials currently have only 13% of the disposal income available to gamble.
- Casinos & games that have been targeted specifically for millennials have failed.
- Millennials propensity for casino gambling is no different from the same AGE-GROUP 50 years ago.

There absolutely is NO objective evidence to support the idea that there's anything unusual about millennials in terms of their propensity for casino gambling. NONE; ZERO.

If a casino is experiencing shortfalls in gaming revenue, objectively it has nothing to do with "millennials". More likely it is a marketing or other issue.

Genuine opportunities may exist to expand gaming revenue with new types of games & betting; but it is incremental revenue not replacement revenue.

Millennials don't gamble because they are not YET in the demographic, income bracket, or psychographic of casino players. When they grow into that demographic, casinos need to be ready for them.

Casinos MUST focus on the core demographic of gamblers; that demographic is not shrinking — it is actually increasing as Generation X and Millennials age into it.

The "Millennial Problem" is NOT based on data; it is purely imagined.

THERE IS NO MILLENNIAL PROBLEM; **the problem is failure to use data.**

Part 5: Making a Brand Great
From Loyalty to Revenue Projections

According to Nielsen's Global New Product Innovation Survey, 59% of the population makes decisions based on Brand, regardless of cost differences. That is exactly the Cheerios-versus-Millville model.

Data indicates that when we combine that innate Branding advantage with over-the-top customer service, the preference decision jumps to 82%; again, regardless of paying a premium price. It is exactly the model of my Delta Airlines decisions.

Building a Brand to those levels requires a series of carefully executed steps. The single most important of those steps is the very first one:

1. **Determine your Brand's target audience.**

As that Cheshire Cat advised, we start at the beginning. Our 20-questions, the RFM modeling, and the look at panic over the aging Baby Boomer market; were all part of that process. And that gives us the foundation we need to transform the Brand to that much-talked-about revenue machine.

2. **Establish a Brand mission.**

What is the value-proposition that we want the Brand to exude? What is the differentiator? What is the market disruptor?

3. **Research competing Brands within your niche.**

What are the big Brands doing? Who are the direct competitors? What are those competitors' messages and visuals? What is their quality of service? Who is talking about them? What marketing are they doing? What makes any of their Brands stand out?

4. **Outline the key qualities & benefits your Brand offers.**

What products, services, and benefits can belong solely to your property? Given the determined target, what gives them a reason to choose your Brand over another?

It's important to note that this is not just a laundry list of the features; it is an analysis of actual benefits.

5. Create a Brand logo & tagline.

The tagline will be what you are known for (like the Rolling Hills' "California's Friendliest Casino"). It needs to be consistent and on everything. The logo is an instant visual that identifies what the Brand is all about (this takes a concentrated creative process to generate).

6. Form your Brand voice.

Based on your target audience and your mission, this is how you communicate with your customers.

It is the style and tone of communications (Friendly? Formal? Folksy? Subservient? Authoritative?); it is what resonates with the target audience. It is also the median that best matches the target audience (personal contact, direct mail, email, Twitter, Facebook, and so on).

7. Build a Brand message & elevator pitch.

Succinctly tell customers who you are, what you offer, and why they should care. It is an emotional communication that people feel is a direct communication with them and not just a slogan. This short message is NOT what your casino does, why it is important to your customer.

8. Integrate your Brand into every aspect of your business.

The Brand is not an occasional presentation; it should be visible and reflected in everything that customers see, read, or hear. It is reflected in both environmental and personal interactions.

9. Make your Brand message believable.

Customers need to believe the viability of your Brand.

When I was Vice President of Marketing and Player Development for Trump, we decided to test the believability of our direct mail pieces. We sent near identical letters to two identical segments of the data base. The only difference was one segment received a letter signed by Donald J. Trump and the other segment received a letter signed by Gary Green.

The Trump letter pulled a 3½% response rate and the one signed by me pulled a 26% response rate.

Baffled by the failure of the Branding to out-perform the unknown signature, we put together focus groups to explore why we received the lopsided seven-times response. We discovered that almost no one believed that the famous Donald Trump had sent them a personal letter; even though the letter contained a monetary offer, it was considered junk mail.

On the other hand, almost everyone thought that the unknown Gary Green was probably a real person who had taken the time to send them a personal letter to get them to come back into the casino.

Moreover, for months afterwards, customers who had trouble at the property would "threaten" casino staff with some equivalent of "I am a personal friend of Gary Green; he writes me letters. Unless you want me to report you to him, then you had better resolve this."

Even a strong Brand like Trump (was at that time) must be constantly monitored and fine-tuned. Similar to other once-great casino Brands that failed, without a constant-focus on the messaging, the consistency

The Brand message MUST be believable.

10. Stay true to your Brand building.

Consistency is essential. Repeat your Brand message constantly. Put it everywhere. Have everything positive associated with it. Create a company culture around the Brand. Inconsistency will confuse your customers.

A Brand crafted with these parameters is ready for the transition from loyalty to revenue. That transition is almost automatic once the Brand has reached this point.

We know, factually and based on historical data, that every casino that has implemented this Branding strategy combined with the RFM marketing strategy has increased revenue by at least 40% the first year. If we apply that proven standard to a hypothetical casino property, we can see exactly how the formulas play out.

Let's create a moderate-size casino with 1,000 slots, six tables, a buffet, a bar, a steakhouse, and a 200-room hotel. Based on comparables and history, let's say the hypothetical slot machine win-per-unit-per-day is $225.

With focused RFM marketing and established Branding we can count on a minimum increase the first year of 40%; giving us a win-per-unit-per-day of $315.

For our hypothetical casino, this gives us annual gross slot machine revenue of $114,975,000.

$315	win per unit per day
1,000	number of machines
$315,000	gross daily revenue
$114,975,000	gross annual revenue

In this hypothetical casino-hotel example, we can assume that we are not buying slot machines; so, they are either on a revenue-share lease (or bucket purchase) for the equivalent of 20% of win-per-unit. To that we will add another 5% to cover premium titles as well as our back-of-the-house systems[10].

That gives us $86,231,250 in slot revenue before we add operating expenses (OPEX) for the entire property; all business units and infrastructure.

$28,743,750	25% games & systems
$86,231,250	pre OPEX revenue

Managing the OPEX for a casino-hotel-resort property is a complex undertaking with management techniques and philosophies all over the place. Even if management adopts the Zero-Based-Budgeting technique, determining the line-item formulas for that technique requires intricate adjustments and handling of the day-to-day operations and overall strategy.

Keeping such hard-core accounting functions within the parameters of the Brand —especially if Delta-style over-the-top customer service is part of the Brand strategy— is a highly-specialized multifaceted function. In my company, Gary Green Gaming™, we do a property-specific analysis that is matched to the goals

---

[10] With the right management in place, rather than an additional expense, the systems might be paid by a charge-back to the various slot vendors for a "connection fee" to the system. This however is a management methodology and not a formulaic decision.

and target of the Brand. From that we create a proprietary line-item strategy for each individual property. That way, the ZBB strategy is matched to the Brand and to the property itself.

In this hypothetical example, I applied our actual formula for a real Tribal casino that implemented our system. That casino matches, very closely, the hypothetical property I described above; including the number of games and win-per-unit. Using those formulas with our $86,231,250 revenue from the example casino, we project ZBB-derived OPEX to be $58,637,250.

That leaves us $27,594,000 EBITDA; a *very* healthy number for that size property.

Again, this methodology must be tied to the specifics of the Brand management itself.

The Branding Paradigm for Revenue

As we have seen, the key to making these formulas work is the entire process of strategic Brand management. The over-performance of this entire revenue model is dependent on the customer developing a relationship with the Brand as the symbol of differentiation from competitors.

This requires that the Brand move from recognition and even awareness to that "*the* versus *MY*" stage of loyalty. To accomplish this, we have to move beyond standard marketing to some seriously-advanced manipulation of customer attitudes.

Rather than simply create a Brand and focus everything the casino does around the Brand, management has to position the Brand to create customer perceptions of the property. This is a HUGE difference.

That level of manipulation involves six areas of strategic Brand management; all of which must personify the Brand:

1. **The physical logo of the Brand.** This is the visual of the brand that is triggered in customers' (and non-customers') minds when the brand name is mentioned.

2. **The style & personality of the Brand.** This is a specific style of writing, color schemes, or a character / person to animate the Brand.

3. **The culture & values of the Brand** is a specific "flavor" or culture tied to the Brand; short of a personification, it is more like a theme that is carried throughout the property.

4. **The relationship with the Brand** is that "red carpet" treatment that Delta provides Diamond travelers. It requires employees of the property to personally interact with the customers. Most importantly, it takes the establishment of a

personal connection between the customer and the property's representative(s).

5. **The consumer identification with the Brand.** The goal is for the specific targeted base customer (determined from the previous formulas) to see a reflection of their own life in the brand. It is designed so that consumers think "this brand is for people just like me" (or, just like they want to be).

6. **The self-image of Brand loyalty** is how consumer perceive that *other consumers* view users of the brand. For example, the perceptions about a consumer who drives a *Ferrari* are different from a consumer who drives a *Chevy Pickup Truck*; or a person who stays at a *Four Seasons Hotel* contrasted to a frequent guest at *Motel 6.*

This euphemistic "Brand positioning" is actually a carefully plotted consumer manipulation to control consumer behavior. Using the Brand as a multi-purpose tool, we can create loyalty and financial value.

What makes a Brand truly great?

Converting the Brand from a name or a logo into a precision financial tool!

Other Books By Gary Green
(available from Amazon and other fine booksellers)

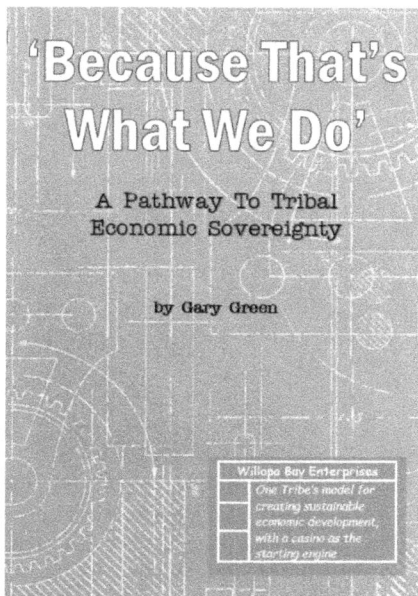

'Because That's What We Do'

A Pathway To Tribal
Economic Sovereignty

by Gary Green

Willapa Bay Enterprises
One Tribe's model for creating sustainable economic development, with a casino as the starting engine

Because That's What We Do — A Pathway To Tribal Economic Sovereignty • <u>Penny Arcades Press</u> • This book is a blueprint for the strategic planning of Tribe-to-Tribe economic development partnerships. While it tells the success-story of the Willapa Bay Enterprises (WBE) Corporation of the Shoalwater Bay Indian Tribe, it actually is a handbook for intertribal processes to transform strained low-income Tribal enterprises into modern successful economic engines.

The backstory is a common one; a Tribal history wrought with struggle, an under-performing casino, misfired businesses, but with Tribal leaders who are eager to take care of their people and build prosperity.

In a novel-perfect plot twist, it all turns around when the right team comes together and creates not only incredible success but a template for sharing the success with other Tribes.

Once the story plays out, the stage is set for a cookie-cutter roadmap to success; a formula that almost any Tribe can duplicate by partnering with WBE.

This book outlines how that partnership works.

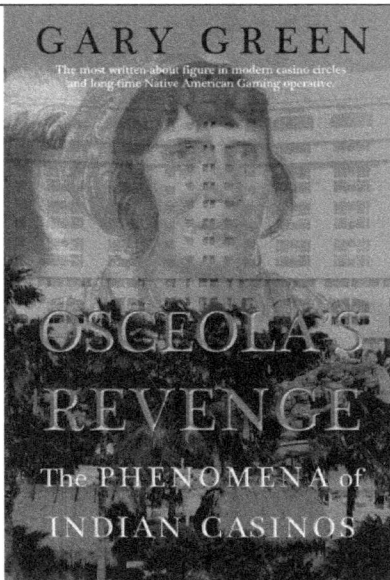

Osceola's Revenge — The Phenomena of Indian Casinos • Brick Tower Press • from an Amazon reviewer: *"This book presents a mostly unknown history of the creation of Native American Casinos. Find out how they work and the issues they have had to deal with. Gary Green is a very knowledgeable casino innovator and historian presenting a subject he has been deeply involved in. His experience includes being a GM of several Native American owned casinos including being on one of Trumps casino management teams. Very interesting read."*

Crossroaders, Georges, & Sporting Men •

Penny Arcades Press • "This biography covers the ex-hilarating life of one of the most colorful and inter-est-ing casino bosses ever: Gary Green." **— Carbon Poker**

David Weischadle, House of Cards: "If you want to know about casinos and the gaming business, you go to one guy, and that guy is Gary Green."

Terrence Nash, ADI News: "A no-holds barred depiction of Green's escapades in the world of casino op-erations, dating as far back as the last days of Meyer Lansky's gambling empire up to the author's stint as a Donald Trump casino marketing executive. After all, Gary Green is well recognized as a seasoned casino manager who

practices his profession by utilizing business analytics, risk assessments, predictive modeling and up-and-coming technologies in improving the organization, funding and performance of modern casino businesses."

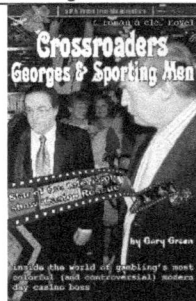

4th and 30; When Journalism Counted • Penny Arcades Press • It is real. It Happened. And it mattered. There used to be something called JOURNALISM. It was a noble "Fourth Estate". There was no concept of anything called "fake news". Cronkite was the "most trusted man in America" and the Times & Post were paragons of integrity. Newspapers were actually "a thing".

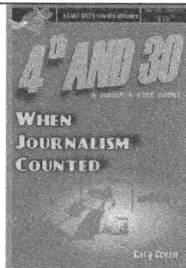

Add to that landscape: axe murders; international monetary manipulation; a small-town police department; Congressional corruption; insane religious cults; cover ups; con men; assassinations; and the ugly zeitgeist of Southern racism.

In a city with the highest per-capita murder rate in the country, Gary Green often arrived on the scene before the cops. Known for unorthodox hands-on reporting that took readers into and behind the scenes, his life was filled with shoot-outs, drug raids, high-speed chases, and every manner of blood and gore. His colorful exploits led to an international mystery of entanglements that made Moriarty look like a piker.

These Six Strings Neutralize The Tools Of Oppression (1976); *Allegory* (1977); *Still At Large* (1980). http://www.folkways.si.edu/search/Gary-Green

Gary Green's three legendary albums originally recorded for the highly-prestigious Folkways Records but re-released by the Smithsonian Institution in Washington DC. Available directly from the Smithsonian or from Amazon, iTunes Store, and other music markets.

		Gambling Man *Pay No Attention To The Man Behind The Curtain* **Marketing-Driven Casino Operational Business Plan** *Marketing Donald Trump*		

Follow Gary Green on Social Media

ABOUT THE AUTHOR

Gary Green one of the country's leading casino developers, operators, and marketers as well as the much-publicized star of the under-development network television series *"Casino Rescue"*. He is author of the book "Osceola's Revenge — The Phenomena of Indian Gaming", and one of the most written-about figures in modern casino gaming.

A former vice president of Trump Hotels & Casino Resorts, during the past 40 years Gary Green, himself, has become one of the casino industry's iconic brands and has worked in or managed almost every operating department inside a modern casino hotel resort.

He has been active in the struggle for Native sovereignty since the early 1970's; long before the Indian Gaming Regulatory Act.

Primarily known for his cutting-edge marketing technologies and creative programs, he also is widely-recognized as one of the casino world's most knowledgeable executives in every aspect of operations, strategic planning, and business modeling. Just in the past year he has been quoted in The New York Times, The Boston Globe, The Newark Star-Ledger, The Los Angeles Times, CNBC, Bloomberg, Yahoo Finance, the official NASDAQ news feed, countless trade publications, and scores of syndicated and local radio and television news programs.

In addition to "Osceola's Revenge", he is the author of "Because That's What We Do — A Pathway To Tribal Economic Sovereignty"; the best-selling book "Gambling Man" (soon to be a major motion picture); as "Marketing Donald Trump"; the textbook "Marketing-Driven Casino Operational Business Plans"; and the upcoming 2019 "Crossroaders, Georges, and Sporting Men" (which reached "best-seller" status in pre-orders).

Gary Green™ is one of only a few casino executives colorful enough to be memorialized in the prestigious Smithsonian Institution, have tens of thousands of Twitter and LinkedIn followers and Facebook fans, registered in IMDB (Internet Movie Database), listed in the Wikipedia online encyclopedia, and have two Pulitzer Prize nominations, along with a string of other honors and awards.

He has spent more than four decades in the casino and entertainment industry in roles from marketing to CEO. He has served on the Board of Directors of the publicly-traded Atlantis Internet Group; on the board of the Las Vegas based Association of Gaming Equipment Manufacturers (AGEM); on the Board of privately-held Hotel Smart Rooms, Inc., and of Tenare Record Corporation; and he is the former owner of the world-renowned EuroCircus.

Gary Green is a walking compendium of vast and varied cross-industry expertise from technology to entertainment to real estate, journalism, franchising, tourism, and (of course) casino gaming.

Gary Green™ is represented by CMA of Beverly Hills of New York, London, and Toronto.

www.GaryGreenGaming.com